Masters of Music

THE WORLD'S GREATEST COMPOSERS

The Life and Times of

Wolfgang Amadeus Mozart

Mitchell Lane
PUBLISHERS

P.O. Box 196
Hockessin, Delaware 19707

Masters of Music

THE WORLD'S GREATEST COMPOSERS

Titles in the Series

The Life and Times of...

Visit us on the web: www.mitchelllane.com
Comments? email us: mitchelllane@mitchelllane.com

Masters of Music

THE WORLD'S GREATEST COMPOSERS

The Life and Times of

Wolfgang Amadeus Mozart

by John Bankston

Printing   5   6   7   8   9

Library of Congress Cataloging-in-Publication Data
Bankston, John, 1974-
       The life and times of Wolfgang Amadeus Mozart / John Bankston.
                     p. cm. — (Masters of music. World's greatest composers)
Summary: Examines the life of the eighteenth-century Austrian composer, from his acclaim as a child prodigy through his prolific musical career to his early death in 1791 at age thirty-five. Includes bibliographical references (p.   ) and index.
       ISBN 1-58415-180-3 (library bound)
    1. Mozart, Wolfgang Amadeus, 1756-1791—Juvenile literature. 2. Composers—Austria—Biography—Juvenile literature. [1. Mozart, Wolfgang Amadeus, 1756-1791. 2. Composers.] I. Title. II. Series.
       ML3930.M9 B25 2003
       780'.92--dc21

                                                                          2002011060
ISBN-13: 9781584151807

ABOUT THE AUTHOR: Born in Boston, Massachusetts, John Bankston has written over three dozen biographies for young adults profiling scientists like Jonas Salk and Alexander Fleming, celebrities like Mandy Moore and Alicia Keys, great achievers like Alfred Nobel, and master musicians like Franz Peter Schubert. An avid reader and writer, he has had a lifelong love of music history. He has worked in Los Angeles, California as a producer, screenwriter and actor. Currently he is in pre-production on *Dancing at the Edge*, a semi-autobiographical film he hopes to film in Portland, Oregon. Last year he completed his first young adult novel, *18 to Look Younger*.

PHOTO CREDITS: Cover: Archivo Iconografico, S.A./Corbis; Back Cover: Hulton/Archive p. 6 Hulton/Archive; p. 10 Stock Montage/SuperStock; p. 13 Archivo Iconografico, S.A./Corbis; p. 18 ET Archive, London/SuperStock; p. 20 Mozart Birthplace, Salzburg, Austria/ET Archive, London/SuperStock; p. 23 North Wind Picture Archive; p. 26 Bettmann/Corbis; p. 33 Archivo Iconografico, S.A./Corbis; p. 36 Archivo Iconografico, S.A./Corbis; p. 38 Robbie Jack/Corbis

PUBLISHER'S NOTE: This story is based on the author's extensive research, which he believes to be accurate. Documentation of such research is contained on page 46.

       The internet sites referenced herein were active as of the publication date. Due to the fleeting nature of some web sites, we cannot guarantee they will all be active when you are reading this book.

                                                          PLB2,4,11,37, PLB4

Contents

The Life and Times of
Wolfgang Amadeus Mozart

by John Bankston

* For Your Information

One of the best-known classical composers in history, Wolfgang Amadeus Mozart's talent was recognized early. Although his fame diminished as he grew older, his work didn't. Throughout his life he continued to pen musical pieces which are today celebrated as among the finest compositions of all time.

Pop Star

I t isn't easy today being a music star. And it wasn't any easier more than two centuries ago. Then, as now, audiences judged musicians by their latest work. If it was a hit, they'd wonder if it could ever be topped. If it was a failure, they figured the musician's talent had faded, their time was over.

Of course, popular music 200 years ago was quite different. Often it was composed for aristocrats or royalty, its first performance generally reserved for society's richest members. The period's "pop" music was opera, but this didn't mean composers lacked fans; even in the 1700s, musician's careers were followed by both their admirers and critics.

The hardest part of becoming a "pop star" is the struggle to get there—those long dark days before talent is rewarded. But when a performer's first taste of fame arrives early, the later years can be even more difficult.

That was the case with Wolfgang Mozart.

Wolfgang was an astonishing talent. His father was a respected musician and teacher who published a book on violin technique the year Wolfgang was born. Yet the boy was largely self-taught. He learned by listening, absorbing every note. When he played, he did more than mimic, he assembled bits and pieces from other composers, sampling previous works like a modern disc jockey. As he grew older, he would gain greater fame as a composer, penning an opera when he was only 12.

By that time he had mastered every instrument he had touched—harpsichord, piano, violin, even his own voice. He was writing music when most kids were learning the alphabet. Wolfgang Mozart was a child prodigy.

As a kid he was ahead of his peers. As an adult he was ahead of everyone. Unfortunately, this meant that many of his works failed to find an audience. Some of his most respected compositions were only appreciated years after his death. Wolfgang earned a great deal of money, but it flowed through his fingers like water. Throughout most of his 20s he was broke and struggling. As a six-year-old he'd entertained the crowned heads of Europe. As a 26-year-old he couldn't hold a job. The man considered by many to be the best composer of all time was forced to pay his bills by giving piano lessons to teenage girls.

When Wolfgang Mozart began to get work again, he was so damaged by depression and illness he couldn't enjoy it. Like many of music's brightest stars, his fire burned rapidly. But it was extinguished early. He was only 35 when he died. His corpse was buried in a mass grave, reserved for the very poor.

Yet while he lived and performed over 200 years ago, his story mirrors many of today's pop stars. It is a story of struggle, of an overbearing father and of heartbreak. It is the story of a man who became famous as a child, but was largely ignored as an adult. It is the story of Wolfgang Mozart, the man called Amadeus, who is one of our great composers. ◆

If Wolfgang Mozart sometimes felt like a outcast because of his abilities, it isn't surprising. Child prodigies have always felt different, mainly because they *are* different. Indeed, the word prodigy used to mean "monstrous."

In biblical times, the future King David was described as a prodigy. In the middle ages, small children with exceptional mathematical talent were put on display like dancing chickens, entertaining crowds with their ability. Mozart and his sister were advertised by their father Leopold as "Prodigies of Nature."

So what is a child prodigy?

It's a kid with a specific talent in one area which exceeds not only his or her peers, but most adults as well. Although prodigies have been found in a number of fields, like painting and even writing, most are concentrated in music, mathematics and chess. This is partly because some skills needed for these areas are innate—the child has them almost from birth. Mozart didn't require years of lessons, and most young chess champs are beating their parents soon after being shown how to play the game.

Of course, prodigies still have to practice, no matter how natural their talent might seem. It helps that most of them enjoy practicing—indeed as a child Wolfgang actually used music in his play. Whether solving a complex mathematical equation or performing a violin concerto, few prodigies consider it work—even practice is fun.

One thing many prodigies have in common is that while they are very advanced in one area, they often don't mature as quickly as other kids. For example, piano prodigy Erwin Nyiregyhazi couldn't even tie his own shoes until he was 21.

On the other hand, prodigies often have skills beyond their recognized specialty. Mozart was brilliant at languages and wrote letters that were very advanced for his age. And like many children who spend most of their time in the company of those quite older, Mozart was very well-spoken as a child and comfortable around adults.

He often dressed as a miniature adult, in a three-cornered hat and wig. In fact, his appearance was so striking that decades later the famous writer Johann Goethe recalled seeing "the little fellow (Mozart was just seven at the time) with his powdered hair and sword."

By the time he was eight years old, Mozart was a seasoned traveler. Along with his sister and his father, he toured Europe performing before an audience of royalty and the upper crust of society.

CHAPTER 2

Miracle Child

In the town of Salzburg, in what is now Austria, the boy who would one day be known as Amadeus was born. The picturesque village of 10,000 situated beside the Salzach River and surrounded by hills was named for its salt mines. However, Salzburg's greatest claim to fame arrived on January 27, 1756, with the birth of Johannes Christomos Wolfgang Gottlieb Mozart. As a child he was called Wolfgang.

Wolfgang and his sister, Maria Anna—nicknamed Nannerl—were the only two of seven children born to Leopold and Anna Maria Mozart to live past infancy. To lose so many children, so young, was tragic but not uncommon in the 18th century. Still, the boy—the Mozarts' seventh and last child—was looked upon immediately as a blessing, a gift from God.

How much of a gift was quickly evident.

Leopold came from a family of bookbinders, a craft that required equal parts of creativity and labor. But his heart wasn't in it. He wanted to be a musician. Although embarking on such an unstable profession was an enormous risk, Leopold's talents were quickly recognized. At 24, he was a violinist in the orchestra of the archbishop of Salzburg, Siegmund von Schrattenbach. By the time his son was born, he'd been promoted to assistant music director. Besides his skills as a musician, he was also respected as a teacher; he wrote the book *Violin Method* the year Wolfgang was born—it is still used today.

Leopold Mozart was very talented, but he was not a genius.

His children were. Some believe musical ability can be passed on to offspring, like blue eyes or blond hair. If that was the case, then the two Mozart children inherited talent by the bucketful. For in addition to Leopold's ability, Anna Maria was herself the grand-daughter of a musician.

Over 200 years ago, however, artistic gifts weren't seen as coming from the parents. A talent for painting, for poetry, for music was viewed as a coming straight from God. In the 18th Century, most Europeans believed the ultimate creator was in heaven and the artist's work was seen as an expression from God. This had enormous implications. There was very little of the shy modesty often seen in artists today—how can one be modest about talent from God? Choosing a career in the arts was a calling, like becoming a priest.

If talent did come from God, then the Mozart children were very blessed. Four and a half years older than Wolfgang, Nannerl quickly became an accomplished harpsichord player. This complex instrument, which contains elements of both the piano and the harp, was taught to her by Leopold. But in the beginning, no one taught Wolfgang. He was too young. Instead he watched, barely noticed, as his older sister practiced. Then as soon as she stopped, he would go over and begin to play.

His parents quickly realized that the boy wasn't just fooling around—he was really playing. Not only was he able to pick out a raw melody on his sister's harpsichord by the time he was three, he was able to play what he heard. While this surprised Leopold, he was astonished by his son's next move. In 1761, the boy began scribbling on composition paper. According to violinist Johann Andreas Schachtner, "One day Wolfgang was busy scribbling away. His father asked what he was writing. 'A keyboard concerto,' Leopold reported the boy replying. 'I've nearly finished the first part.'"

Leopold didn't believe it—until he examined the paper. The boy was actually composing, although at the time he could barely write his own name!

There was no question about it. Wolfgang Mozart's gifts surpassed those of his peers, his sister—indeed most adults. Leopold was ready for the next step. A tour!

Composing before he could spell, Wolfgang wrote dozens of compositions before he was a teenager.

Music tours didn't originate with today's rock stars and pop acts. They have been going on for centuries. Leaving their hometown, traveling on unfamiliar roads, sleeping in foreign beds and eating strange meals—all these were even more difficult in Mozart's time.

In the 1700s, few musicians were independent professionals. Musicians' employment was at the whim of their employers. These men and women included top clergy members, royalty and wealthy merchants. Any decision the musicians made—whether to travel, what pieces to perform—had to be cleared first.

However, as much as sponsors like the archbishop Leopold worked for demanded obedience, they also appreciated the value of publicity. Today pop stars tour to sell albums. In the 18th Century musicians worked to gain their own level of fame—fame which reflected favorably on their employers. And few things could bring as much fame as a child prodigy. So Archbishop von Schrattenbach was generous in Leopold's increasing requests for time off for travel.

The first tour came in 1762 when Wolfgang traveled with his sister and father to Munich and Vienna. It was only a brief trip, but enough to convince Leopold of the value of touring. It would expose his children's talents to the world, it would give them the opportunity to see other cultures and interact with the top members of European society.

And then there was the matter of money.

Leopold believed that people would flock to the concerts of his two child prodigies. That would produce much more income than he earned in Salzburg.

So in June, 1763, the entire family set off on an extended trip for France and then England. In Paris, the children performed for the

French king and queen and members of the royal court. Then the family crossed the English Channel. They settled in London and spent more than a year there. After they returned to continental Europe, they made several more stops that included another visit to Paris. They finally returned home in November, 1766. They had been gone for nearly three and a half years.

At every stop there were rewards—elegant snuff boxes, well-crafted watches and shiny gold coins. Royals gave the children expensive hand-me-downs. As a youngster, Wolfgang was attired in the finest clothing, along with a powdered wig and a tiny sword. Small for his age, with a large nose and deep-set eyes, he would

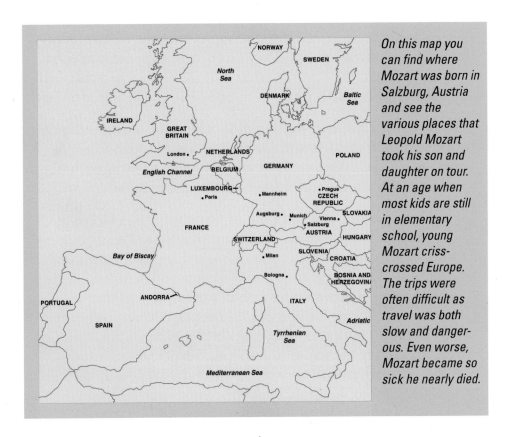

On this map you can find where Mozart was born in Salzburg, Austria and see the various places that Leopold Mozart took his son and daughter on tour. At an age when most kids are still in elementary school, young Mozart criss-crossed Europe. The trips were often difficult as travel was both slow and danger-ous. Even worse, Mozart became so sick he nearly died.

never pass for attractive, but had to settle for "striking." Still, Wolfgang managed to look quite a bit like the offspring of the princes and princesses he tried to entertain.

During their journey, many saw the two children as little more than well-trained pets, no more remarkable than dancing monkeys. A few, however, knew real talent when they saw it, and weren't shy about describing the boy's gifts. In London, for example, Wolfgang befriended Johann Christian Bach. Besides being the son of the famous composer Johann Sebastian Bach, Johann Christian was popular on his own—perhaps the best known composer in England.

Despite the advantages of touring, it had drawbacks as well. Travel in the 18th century was a rough business. Besides bad roads, travelers faced the threat of thieves. Sometimes the carriages in which they rode broke down. They faced large expenses for food and lodging. Often the family shared a single bed—a bed that was likely to be crawling with fleas.

And everywhere there was sickness. The same illnesses that had struck down their siblings still made their way through Europe. Nannerl nearly died from typhoid fever. Wolfgang endured, among other things, a form of scarlet fever and frequent colds.

After nine months at home, the Mozarts went to a wedding party in Vienna. But the bride died from smallpox. The disease was sweeping through the city. Leopold panicked and rushed his children from the area. It was too late. Wolfgang and Nannerl caught the disease, though in a mild form, but its scars would mar Wolfgang's face. While his son was ill, Leopold expressed normal paternal concern. However, once the child recovered, his attention returned to money. He wrote to a friend, "Hypothetically calculated, this little adventure has cost me fifty ducats." So as soon as Wolfgang recovered, Leopold took the family back to Vienna. There were places to play and ducats to earn. ◆

SMALLPOX

The origins of smallpox can be traced to Asia. The disease's ravages, which are often fatal and marked by the pimples or "poxes" which cover the sick person's body, reached Europe about the seventh Century A.D. Some estimates put the number of smallpox cases during the 18th Century at 60,000,000.

Wolfgang and Nannerl were very lucky. The disease left scars, but also left them alive. Many others were not as fortunate. The question of how to survive—or better yet, prevent—this dreadful disease was one which haunted doctors.

The answer came from cows.

Women who milked cows often came in contact with the animal's udder, where "cowpox" sores were present. The disease was harmless to people, and the women who came into contact with the "cowpox" didn't get smallpox. A bright doctor named Edward Jenner noticed this phenomenon and decided to conduct an experiment in 1796.

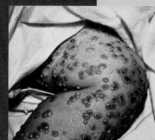

Jenner scraped off some of the cowpox and injected it into an eight-year-old boy. The boy got sick, but recovered. Six weeks later, the doctor injected the same boy with smallpox sores. Nothing happened. The boy was now immune to smallpox. This meant he could no longer get sick from the disease.

It was the first time this method was used, and it paved the way for a variety of shots designed to protect us from getting other illnesses. Dr. Jenner even came up with the name for this method. Using "vacca," the Latin word for cow, he called the technique vaccination.

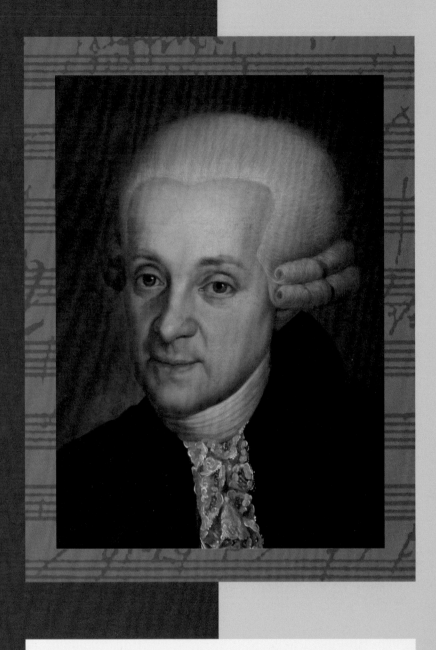

Although Leopold Mozart was talented enough to earn a top job and publish a respected book on violin technique, he never achieved his dreams. Instead he relentlessly pushed his children, hoping they could lead the life he'd never been able to.

CHAPTER

3

Getting Tested

I f Leopold Mozart was to be compared to a 21st Century character type, it would be the stage mother. Like the stereotypes of these over-involved parents, pushing their children to perform and often pocketing their earnings, Leopold was a heavy presence in his children's lives. Sure, they loved music, loved the audience, but the price they paid for their talent was years away from home and little time for childish indulgences.

While many saw Leopold as a hardworking father, simply trying to expose the world to his children's gifts, he didn't convince everyone. Many quietly questioned his judgment as a parent, the way he promoted his children. He once asked an acquaintance named Johann Adolph Hasse for a recommendation to an important man in Italy. Hasse wrote the letter praising Wolfgang's talents but added, "The father, so far as I can see, is eternally discontented with everything. Here too complaints are being made about this. He idolizes his son a thought too much, and does everything possible to spoil him."

Wolfgang could be obnoxious. He made vulgar jokes and as he approached his teens still behaved like a kid. Yet for the most part, his work required him to be like an adult—there was little time for him to be otherwise.

Despite, or perhaps because of this maturity, he often begged for affection—asking even royalty for kisses and hugs. He asked everyone if they loved him, and if they said no, even jokingly, he cried. For Wolfgang, the life of a pre-teen musician could be a very lonely one.

But even in sadness, Wolfgang had his music. He played instruments with the talent of someone much older, and his main love quickly became composing. In the beginning, much of what he

Sometimes vulgar, often spoiled teenage Mozart was so talented he got away with all kinds of bad behavior. As he grew older, others were less tolerant which caused him some serious problems.

wrote mimicked the popular melodies of the times. But quite quickly, his own style became distinctive.

When he was 12, Wolfgang Mozart was able to try his hand at one of the most demanding musical forms: the opera. His father spurred him to the effort, believing it would bring new attention to his son's talent.

Wolfgang was up to the challenge.

Opera is a musical style where most, and frequently all, of the dialogue is sung rather than spoken—somewhat like modern musicals. Combining emotion and drama, opera would have been very familiar to any youth in Mozart's time, especially one as widely traveled as he was. He'd seen a number of the best works, and prior to puberty even his voice was an instrument: Wolfgang had perfect pitch. This means he didn't need to hear a note in order to sing it perfectly.

So while the family was in Vienna in 1768, Wolfgang wrote a comedic opera, *La Finta Semplice* (The Pretend Simpleton). Those who heard the work usually had one of two reactions. They were amazed, or they were threatened.

Adult opera writers who'd been working for years were worried about this upstart. They conspired against him and managed to keep the work from being performed for over a year. Wolfgang was devastated. Fortunately he didn't have to suffer for long. A wealthy doctor named Franz Anton Mesmer paid him to write a small opera for his own private theater.

So the first public showing of a Wolfgang Mozart opera occurred at Dr. Mesmer's theater on October 1, 1768 with the premiere of *Bastien and Bastienne*.

In 1769, the family returned to Salzburg. Wolfgang was something of a conquering hero—a local boy who'd made good. *La Finta Semplice* was performed at the Archbishop's palace. While his father returned to his old position, Wolfgang's reward was an appointment as concertmaster with the Archbishop's orchestra.

But there were concerts to give, tours to take, money to be made. So in December, 1769, Leopold and Wolfgang set out for Italy.

Nannerl didn't accompany her father and brother this time. At the age of 18 she didn't qualify as a child prodigy any longer. So she stayed behind with her mother.

Always a joker, Wolfgang sent her a little note that promised her "a hundred kisses or slaps on your great horseface."

Leopold knew Italy would be perfect for Wolfgang. The country was a center for opera production; most operas were written in Italian. Wolfgang's attraction to the country was immediate and powerful. At one opera, overtaken by the wonder of it all, he exclaimed, "What fun!"

Not only did he embrace Italian music and culture, he even began signing his letters "Amadeo" or "Amadé," which was Italian for Gottlieb, his middle name. Only much later would he be referred to by Amadeus, the Latin version. Translated into English, the name means "beloved of God." In Italy, Amadeo was beloved of everyone.

Professionally, Italy offered the teenage Mozart a variety of opportunities. He gave concerts of his own compositions, and was hired to compose his first dramatic opera.

Besides a growing career, his talents were rewarded in other ways as well. Pope Clement IV made him a Knight of the Golden

Spur, an extraordinary honor for someone his age. In the Northern Italian town of Bologna he was examined by the Accademia Filarmonica for admission. Locked in a room, he was expected to complete a difficult composition. The test was usually given to musicians in their 20s, who would take about four hours to complete it.

Wolfgang Mozart walked out of the room less than an hour later. He passed.

As a young boy, Wolfgang played for members of royalty, such as Empress Maria Theresa seen here. When he was older, he felt confident she would give him a recommendation for a job, and was shocked when she refused.

Besides the examination, Mozart also had his skills tested in Bologna by Padre Giovanni Battista Martini, who'd taught Johann Christian Bach. Leopold called Martini "the idol of the Italians." Here was someone with something to teach Wolfgang: counterpoint. This difficult technique involves the blending or mixing of several melodies, and includes the fugue—the hardest aspect of counterpoint to master. Indeed, Wolfgang would make little use of the lessons at first. But by the time he was in his 30s, counterpoint would be a prime ingredient in his work. Martini was impressed with Wolfgang, and years later would defend him relentlessly.

In 1771, Leopold's employer, the Archbishop von Schrattenbach, died. His replacement, the Count Hieronymus Colloredo, was not as lenient. He demanded that Leopold and Wolfgang return to Salzburg permanently or lose their jobs. The two didn't obey immediately.

Leopold contacted Ferdinand, the son of Austria's empress, Maria Theresa. Because Wolfgang had written a musical composition for Ferdinand's wedding, surely his mother would be willing to help the boy get a job.

She wasn't. She refused to write a recommendation for him, and added in a response to her son's request, "It lowers the tone when such people roam the world like beggars." Clearly she was not impressed with Leopold or his offspring. Wolfgang next tried to get a position in Vienna, a city that would later become increasingly important to him. He was no more successful than his father had been.

Disappointed, Wolfgang returned to his home town late in 1773. He wasn't happy. ◆

VIENNA

The site of present-day Vienna was established about 800 B.C. during the Bronze Age. The Romans occupied it in the first Century A.D. and named it Vindobona. It became an important site for defending the northern frontier of the Roman Empire.

It lost importance when the Roman Empire collapsed, but eventually was rebuilt into an important trading center by 1100. By then it was known as Wenia. Eventually it became the capitol of the vast Hapsburg empire.

Its university, the oldest in the German-speaking world, was founded in 1365. During the Renaissance (1400-1600), the city became a leader in the arts and education. In the 1500s conflict came to the city, as the Turks began a series of wars that lasted for nearly 150 years. In 1679 the bubonic plague killed nearly a third of the city's residents.

By Mozart's childhood, war and disease were not issues. Palaces and huge mansions had been built in the early part of the 18th century, and the Linienwall protected the suburbs. Factories and the re-emergence of the arts in this city of over 175,000 drew immigrants from across Europe. Vienna's arts reflected their influence. For an aspiring composer like Wolfgang Mozart, it was a magical place, bustling with activity and the types of creative inspiration he craved.

During the time known as the Classical Period, three great composers besides Wolfgang called Vienna home. Franz Joseph Haydn, a famous composer whose work was a great influence on Mozart, lived there during Wolfgang's time. The two men met, and in 1785 Haydn told Mozart's father that "Before God and as an honest man I tell you that your son is the greatest composer known to me either in person or by name." Ludwig van Beethoven and Franz Schubert would soon follow.

Empress Maria Theresa, so unhelpful to Mozart, brought about compulsory primary school attendance, separated the university from the church, and reorganized the city's economy. Her son Joseph II continued these reforms. By the time of Mozart's death, the city had grown to over 235,000 inhabitants.

Talented and spoiled, beautiful sixteen-year old Aloysia Weber was the perfect match for 21-year-old Wolfgang. Too perfect. While she was just having fun, he was falling in love. After their break-up, he married her sister.

CHAPTER

4

In and Out of Love

Mozart hated Salzburg. He found the town boring, especially after the excitement of Milan, London, Vienna and all the other great cities he'd seen. Besides the lack of thrills, Wolfgang was 17. Like most teens, he was ready to be on his own and tired of living beneath the watchful gaze of his parents. Leopold had dictated much of the way Wolfgang spent his life, but this time he began to rebel.

The rebellion was a slow process. Life was different in the 18th century. Unmarried men and women often lived with their parents until well into their 20s, and were expected to obey without question.

Wolfgang didn't want to stay in his hometown, he wanted to tour, he wanted to compose operas. But unlike his father, Wolfgang wasn't motivated by money. He wanted to meet girls.

Unfortunately, he had a job. Although his father tried to get the teen a better position, he was unsuccessful. So, Wolfgang returned to working for Salzburg's archbishop, just like his dad. In idle moments, the younger Mozart must have wondered if he would share his father's fate—decades of service to an unappreciative boss,

creative decline and a gradual sinking into anonymity. After all, Wolfgang was independent, creative, stubborn.

In other words, a terrible employee.

So, even as he continued to write for the church—composing over half a dozen symphonies in just a few months—he continued to seek opportunities elsewhere. In 1775, he and his father took what would be their last trip together. The pair went to Munich, for the premiere of *La Finta Giardiniera* (The Pretend Gardener), a comic opera Wolfgang had written. Afterwards, despite Salzburg's lack of charm for the composer, he continued to be enormously productive, penning a number of other pieces, including four concertos for piano and another five for the violin.

Finally in 1777, Wolfgang had had enough. He quit. He was ready to strike out on his own, earning money composing for whomever would hire him. It was an uncommon choice in the 18th century where most artists relied on the steady work provided by archbishops and wealthy patrons.

Leopold was worried. "You must devote all your attention to earning some money," he would later advise his son. He recognized Wolfgang's frivolous tendencies and didn't want him tramping across Europe—even if he was 21. Leopold wanted to go with him, keep an eye on him. But when he asked Archbishop Colloredo if he could take some time off, the archbishop told him he could take all the time he wanted, but there wouldn't be a job waiting when he came back. Reluctantly, Leopold stayed at his job.

Wolfgang was a grown man, and excited by the prospects of his first European tour on his own. However, Leopold still had one more weapon in his arsenal, that age-old parental sword: guilt.

So, instead of a father as traveling partner, Mozart got his mother. The two journeyed to Munich together. Soon afterward,

they stopped over in nearby Augsburg, staying with relatives of Leopold's. If he'd thought giving Wolfgang a maternal chaperone and only relatives to keep him company would reduce the composer's natural curiosity, he was wrong.

Wolfgang Mozart just kept it in the family.

Anna Maria Thekla was his first cousin. She was also his first girlfriend. Nineteen years old, she could be as rowdy as Wolfgang, and unlike most women of the time, didn't shock easily. "My little cousin is pretty, bright, charming. We get on really well, for like myself, she is a bit of a rascal," he wrote his father.

Leopold wasn't happy. He didn't feel his son was financially capable of supporting a family, and didn't want him to lose his focus. He would have been even unhappier if he'd seen the letters Mozart penned to his younger cousin, such as the one he penned in French, writing, "I long to kiss your hands, your face, your knees, and your — in short, all you permit me to kiss."

Leopold wasn't taking any chances. He ordered Wolfgang to go to the city of Mannheim. Leopold expected him to find regular work there. Instead, Wolfgang fell in love.

His interest in his cousin had been experimental. His interest in Aloysia Weber was far deeper. The 16-year-old daughter of an impoverished musician, she was both beautiful and talented. She dreamed of becoming a professional singer. Wolfgang dreamed of becoming her husband.

Aloysia wasn't very serious about young Mozart, but he was very serious about her. He imagined rescuing her from her poverty, writing her the most beautiful songs and sponsoring her on a European tour. He would abandon his dreams for hers. But Wolfgang made the mistake of including his idle fantasies in a letter home.

"You must with all your soul think of your parent's welfare, otherwise your soul will go to the devil," Leopold angrily wrote back, reminding his child about his financial obligations. Then, in February of 1778, the tone was unmistakable: "Off with you to Paris."

Not only did Wolfgang not want to go to Paris, his mother didn't either. Anna Maria was not the seasoned traveler her husband had been. She wanted to go home to Salzburg. She was tired of traveling. But her husband was as demanding of her as he'd been of Wolfgang. Leopold insisted she go with her son to Paris; he was certain the young man needed a chaperone.

This was a mistake.

Paris became a struggle. Wolfgang played to disinterested audiences and steady work was rare. He was forced to give lessons on the clavier, an early form of the piano. He loathed teaching because he was convinced it interfered with his composing.

His mother's time in Paris was just as difficult. She spent most of the day alone in a windowless room, waiting for her son. In June of 1778 she became ill, and slipped into a coma. She died on July 3rd. Wolfgang was devastated—but not enough to return home.

"Salzburg is not the place for my talents!" he wrote his father.

Paris didn't seem to be the place for them either. Wolfgang's money was running out. In September, after getting a loan from a Parisian patron, he followed his heart. He traveled on a slow carriage to Mannheim, only to learn that Aloysia was in Munich. It took him two more months to get there. She was a celebrated soprano, an ambitious girl with few interests beyond her career. When Wolfgang saw her, he quickly told her his feelings. Aloysia looked at him coldly. Her love for him had been a fantasy of his creation, as intricate as any composition. In just a few months he lost both his mother and the woman he dreamed of marrying. Once again the composer buried his pain in writing. He composed for the object of his misdirected desire a beautiful aria. "People of Thessaly," designed specifically for Aloysia's voice, was his last romantic gesture before he left Munich.

Salzburg was grabbing Wolfgang like a lake devouring a drowning man. Leopold's demands were becoming overwhelming. In January of 1779, the composer returned to Salzburg. Reluctantly, Wolfgang signed a new contract with the archbishop. He was to be court organist—earning three times what he'd made as a concertmaster.

It wasn't enough. Wolfgang found diversions from his job, writing symphonies and even a double concerto he and his sister could play together. In the summer of 1780 he wrote *Idomeneo* for Munich's Carnival. Many people consider it to be his first great opera.

However, working for the archbishop was brutal. For Colloredo, it was all about control. In March of 1781, Wolfgang was enjoying *Idomeneo*'s premiere in Munich when the archbishop summoned him to Vienna, where he was staying for the coronation of Joseph II, the new emperor. He wanted Wolfgang to perform at various functions in Joseph's honor. Ordered about, Wolfgang felt overworked and underpaid. Worse, during a meal in Vienna he was seated with the servants—an incredible act of disrespect toward a man who'd performed for royalty. "At least, I have the honor of sitting ahead of the cooks," he joked.

There was no joking with Archbishop Colloredo. Despite his religious position, he was easy with the insult and called Wolfgang a "scoundrel" or a "rogue" right to his face. Finally, Wolfgang couldn't take it any more. He quit—this time for good. He was 23 and it was the last time he'd hold a steady job. His father urged him to reconsider, but Wolfgang angrily wrote back, "if I have to go begging, I no longer want to serve such a master."

His timing wasn't the best. The Austrian and Turkish empires were engaged in a costly war. Economic conditions didn't favor a musician trying to make a living on his own.

But Wolfgang was very proud. He was also very broke. He took a room in a boarding house run by Aloysia Weber's mother. By now the object of his affections had married another man—an actor—and her father had died. The widowed mother settled in Vienna and operated the boarding house with the aid of her other daughters.

Aloysia might not have been available, but her sister was. Constanze was barely 19, and although a trained musician she was neither as talented nor as ambitious as her sister had been. For Wolfgang this must have looked like a good thing. When he wrote his father about the situation, Leopold was appalled. His letters back to his son consisted of attacks on Constanze and unfounded rumors about her behavior. Wolfgang ignored his father's complaints, and in December of 1781, admitted that he planned on marrying the woman.

"Nature speaks in me as loudly as in anyone, and perhaps louder than in many big, strong lungs," he explained.

Money was, as always, an issue. Wolfgang's efforts to get a steady job as court composer in Vienna failed as the position was already held by Antonio Salieri, who was six years older than Wolfgang. Salieri apparently took little comfort in this accomplishment, and despite sharing a double bill with the younger composer in 1786, there were rumors that the two were rivals. Like Mozart,

Salieri was musically accomplished at a young age — he would eventually write over forty-four operas. Unfortunately, he didn't advance from the position of court composer and by the 1790s his music would fall out of favor. Today he's best known as a music teacher who instructed, among others, Beethoven and Schubert.

Constanze Weber was less talented and less ambitious than her sister. But more importantly, she returned Mozart's love and married him despite his lack of a steady job. Even though Mozart faced numerous challenges during the rest of his life, the couple's love endured.

Through the early part of 1782, Wolfgang struggled to complete The Abduction from the Seraglio, a comic opera. It premiered on July 16. Although Joseph II reportedly told Wolfgang afterwards, "Too many notes, dear Mozart," audiences loved it.

The opera was a financial success. Buoyed by this, Wolfgang married Constanze the next month. He was positive the money would begin flowing. He certainly needed it to. Constanze was soon pregnant.

In August 1783, shortly after the birth of their first child, the couple traveled to Salzburg, where Leopold and Nannerl met Constanze for the first time. The infant stayed behind in the care of a nurse. When Wolfgang and his young bride returned to Vienna, they learned their baby had died. Three more of their children would die in infancy. Like his parents, Wolfgang only had two children who lived to adulthood—Karl Thomas, born in 1784, and Franz Wolfgang Xaver, born in 1791.

Grieving over the death of his first child, Wolfgang buried his grief in work as he wrote a series of piano concertos. Meanwhile, he struggled to find patrons—people wealthy enough to finance operas or concerts of his music.

It didn't happen.

Hoping to meet Vienna's elite, Wolfgang joined the Freemasons in December of 1784. For the composer, finding members who would pay for his dreams took a while. His struggles continued.◆

FYInfo
FREEMASONS

"Sacred be this day, O humanity! To advance your well being, two members have attached themselves to the great chain of masons; on the steps of your solemn altar two of your sons have sworn their unbreakable oath that, joined with us, they will devote themselves wholly to virtue and wisdom!"

Those were the words Wolfgang Mozart heard as he was inducted into Beneficence, one of eight Freemasonic lodges in Vienna. It was December 14, 1784 and while the composer may have been interested in the organization's history of good works, he was more concerned with the contacts he would make.

Just as some college students join sororities and fraternities in hopes of furthering future career goals, so Mozart hoped to find nobility among the Masons—nobles who would finance his ventures. What he quickly learned was that while there were monarchs and prime ministers among the members, most of the Freemasons were successful "commoners"—merchants, business people, artists.

And by the time Mozart joined, they were in trouble.

Secret societies, organizations whose practices and ceremonies are only known to members, existed centuries before Mozart's interest. However, the Freemasons attracted more attention than many other societies because of their belief in equality. Royalty in Europe was threatened by many Masonic doctrines, but this idea that all men are equal angered both the royals and the churches. In 1743, Empress Maria Theresa had a lodge raided; her son Joseph II shut down many more of them down.

Still, for Wolfgang, the Freemasons proved profoundly influential. As he quickly rose in their ranks from Apprentice to Fellow to Mason, he began to compose music built around their ceremonies. One of his greatest operas, *The Magic Flute*, was profoundly affected by the organization's ceremonies. Many consider it a truly Masonic opera.

Besides the creative inspiration, in his later, debt-ridden years Wolfgang was always able to count on a fellow Mason for a loan.

His hands so swollen he could barely grasp a quill, Wolfgang composed his final work. The Requiem was written for a funeral and Mozart died just after its completion.

CHAPTER

5

Requiem

L ate one September night in 1791, Constanze and
Wolfgang Mozart were preparing to go to Prague. As the
couple reached their carriage, a figure emerged from the
shadows. He grabbed at Constanze's dress. Looking at Wolfgang,
he demanded, "What will become of the *Requiem?*"

Wolfgang didn't know what to say. The man stood there, his
features concealed beneath a cloak. Missing deadlines was becoming a habit for the composer.

For the most part, Mozart had spent the 1780s productively.
Besides numerous pieces for violin, piano and other instruments,
Wolfgang completed two of his greatest operas. *The Marriage of
Figaro*, which premiered in 1786, and *Don Giovanni*, which opened
the next year, are considered by scholars to be two of the best
operas ever written. They were also far too sophisticated for the
Vienna audiences and failed miserably. Although *Figaro* found a
receptive audience in Prague (in the modern-day Czech Republic),
composers of the time did not earn royalties the way music writers
do today. So Mozart saw little money from his efforts.

To pay the bills, Wolfgang continued to offer private music
lessons for Vienna's elite and their children. While there were

A failure when it was introduced, Don Giovanni is today considered one of the best operas ever written. It is still widely performed, as illustrated by this 2001 show.

rumors about Wolfgang's involvement with several of his young female students, this was never proven.

In 1787, Mozart earned a position as chamber composer for the Viennese court. Although the position was a high honor, it paid poorly.

As his finances grew steadily worse, so did his health. In 1790, Mozart was frequently ill, bedridden from episodes of crippling depression and struggling to make ends meet.

In 1791, new opportunities arrived. By then, Wolfgang was scarcely able to appreciate them.

Fellow Freemason Emanuel Schikaneder got him involved with a comic opera, *The Magic Flute*. The opera featured spoken lines as well as singing. It also revealed secret Masonic ceremonies—an act that the lodge rules said was punishable by death. Because of this, some believed the Masons poisoned Mozart, who spent the last six months of his life increasingly ill. However, considering that nothing happened to Schikaneder, this is unlikely.

Besides *The Magic Flute*, Mozart was on a tight deadline as he completed two other pieces, including an opera written for a king's coronation in Prague. For the first time, he was busy and the money was rolling in.

Then he was visited by the cloaked stranger. Like the man himself, his story is shrouded in mystery. What is known is that in July of 1791, Wolfgang had been hired to write a requiem—music based on the Catholic mass to be played at a funeral. The amount he was offered was tremendous. The cloaked figure claimed to be working for someone else—some believe it was a Viennese noble whose wife had recently died. Because of his various projects and competing deadlines, Wolfgang struggled to keep up. As 1791 dragged on, the composer was consumed.

Leaving for the king's coronation in Prague, Mozart promised the stranger that he would work on the *Requiem* as soon as he returned. His excuses were accepted. A few weeks later, he conducted *The Magic Flute*, which premiered on September 30 in Vienna. But soon he fell so ill he could not continue. The opera eventually ran for over 100 performances—a record in Vienna.

Sadly, Wolfgang Mozart wouldn't live to see its final performance. During the next two months, he struggled to finish the *Requiem*. Writing music for a death convinced Mozart that he was dying himself.

He was right.

He completed two of the *Requiem*'s eight sections and sketched the musical outline of the rest. But on December 4th, his hands were so swollen he couldn't hold a quill. So he discussed the *Requiem* with a young composer named Franz Süssmyer, a student of his. Süssmyer and several others would finish the magnificent work.

For at 1:00 the next morning, resting in his wife Constanze's arms, Wolfgang Mozart died. He was 35 years old and over 600 works bore his name. Despite this, there was no money for a decent funeral, and one of the world's greatest composers was buried in an unmarked grave among the bodies of Vienna's poor.

Constanze wrote a short note to her dead spouse a few days later: "Dearly beloved Mozart—never to be forgotten by me or by the whole of Europe."

She predicted the future. Wolfgang has never been forgotten—not in Vienna nor Salzburg, not in all of Europe, indeed not in the whole world.

Wolfgang Mozart's fame, like that of many great artists, did not truly arrive until after his death. In life he struggled with his finances. In death, his music is performed across the globe for paying audiences that number millions of people every year.

Even Hollywood and pop music have honored the composer.

In 1984, director Milos Forman and writer Peter Shaffer brought their version of his life to the big screen. The movie *Amadeus* focused on the rivalry between Salieri and Mozart. Tom Hulce, the actor who played Mozart, emphasized the composer's immaturity and crude humor even as Salieri questioned how a just God could bless someone so crude with so much talent. The movie won an Oscar for Best Picture. In real life, Salieri went insane in 1823, dying two years later, his reputation destroyed by unfounded rumors that he had murdered Mozart.

Another homage arrived in 1986 when Viennese techno-rap artist Falco imagined the great composer as a modern, punk-haired musician in his hit single and music video "Rock Me Amadeus." Besides repeating the title line over and over, the song's lyrics also gave facts about the composer. Quite a few kids growing up in the 1980s learned details of Mozart's life from this song!

Like the subject of "Rock Me Amadeus," Falco died fairly young. He was killed in a car accident at the age of 40.

And on September 11, 2002, the first anniversary of the terrorist attacks in New York City, the whole world remembered Mozart. At precisely 8:46 a.m. in every time zone around the globe—the moment that the first hijacked airliner plunged into the World Trade Center—orchestras and singers presented what was called the Rolling Requiem for hundreds of thousands of listeners. For nearly a full day, Mozart's *Requiem* was being performed somewhere in the world.

No one could think of a more fitting way to remember the thousands of people who lost their lives on that tragic day.

THE AGE OF ENLIGHTENMENT,
THE AGE OF REASON

Imagine being Wolfgang Mozart, growing up in the middle 1700s. As a musician, he was able to meet some of his era's most famous people. When he was seven, a French noblewoman named Madame de Pompadour refused the lad's request for a peck on the cheek. He exclaimed, "Who does she think she is not wanting to kiss me? Why the empress herself kissed me!"

Young Wolfgang found himself welcomed in royal courts across Europe. He met emperors and empresses, princes and princesses; yet, as he grew older he quickly realized that his position in European society was only a notch or two above servants. The pop stars of today with their five-star hotels and chartered jet lifestyles have little in common with Wolfgang. Even when he stayed in the finest castles, the prodigy endured rooms that were drafty and cold in the winter, stifling hot in the summer. Rats and insects made their homes in the finest palaces and the roofs leaked during storms. The richest nobles seldom bathed, attempting to cover their odors with perfumes and their dirt with powders. Indeed, Wolfgang's father Leopold made note of one Englishman who "at least every other day bathed in the Main and would then come to the table looking like a baptized mouse."

Leopold spent much of their earnings keeping up appearances—traveling by private coaches and staying in reasonable accommodations. But there was little the Mozart family could do to rise above their station. Austria—indeed much of the world—was run by people born into power, not elected to it.

In the late 1700s that began to change.

Wolfgang grew up in the Age of Enlightenment. It was a period when reformers—who included intellectuals and artists—believed the work they did represented the highest ideals of humankind. Centered in Paris, the Enlightenment movement embraced open debate and criticism of those in power, from kings to popes. Some of Mozart's best-known operas, such as *Don Giovanni* and *The Marriage of Figaro*, reflect the influence of the Enlightenment.

In many ways the beliefs of the movement helped inspire revolutionaries in America and later in France. Individualistic artists benefited from changes that followed. Instead of following the orders of a sponsor, they were able to follow their vision. Sadly, many of the reforms the movement encouraged happened long after Mozart's death.

Selected Works

La Finta Semplice (The Pretend Simpleton) – opera

Bastien and Bastienne – opera

La Finta Giardiniera (The Pretend Gardener) – opera

People of Thessaly – aria

Idomeneo – Opera

The Abduction from the Seraglio – A comic opera

The Magic Flute – opera

The Marriage of Figaro – opera

Don Giovanni – opera

The Requiem

Goethe's Das Veilchen (The Violet) Songs, with piano accompaniment.

Symphony No. 29

Symphony No. 31,

Symphonies 35, 36 and 38 The Salzburg Symphonies (generally known in English as Divertimenti, K. 136, 137 and 138.)

Symphony No. 39, in E flat major

Symphony No. 40 in G minor

Symphony No. 41, Jupiter Symphony

Chronology

1756	born in Salzburg, Austria on January 27 to Leopold and Anna Maria Mozart
1761	writes his first composition
1762	begins first tour as he travels with his sister Nannerl and his father to Munich
1763	family leaves Salzburg for three years of touring Europe
1764	meets Johann Christian Bach in London
1767	performs his first piano concertos
1778	first opera is performed
1769	travels with his father to Italy
1770	made Knight of the Golden Spur by Pope Clement IV
1773	returns to Salzburg
1777	leaves on tour to Paris with his mother; falls in love with Aloysia Weber
1778	mother dies
1781	moves to Vienna
1782	marries Constanze Weber
1784	joins Freemasons
1787	father dies
1789	travels to Prague and Berlin
1791	dies in Vienna on December 5

1709	piano invented in Italy by Bartolomeo Cristofori
1750	birth of composer Antonio Salieri, who becomes Mozart's rival
1756	Seven Years War begins (known as French and Indian War in U.S.)
1759	death of composer George Frideric Handel
1761	George III becomes King of England
1763	end of Seven Years War
1766	in the U.S., the Mason-Dixon line is drawn; it eventually becomes dividing line between slave and free states
1769	birth of Napoleon Bonaparte
1770	birth of composer Ludwig van Beethoven
1773	American revolutionaries protesting British taxation dump cargo into Boston Harbor in what becomes known as the Boston Tea Party
1775	Battles of Lexington and Concord, first actions of US Revolutionary War
1776	Signing of Declaration of Independence on July 4 in Philadelphia
1778	British explorer James Cook discovers Hawaii
1781	U.S. troops win Battle of Yorktown, last major battle of Revolutionary War
1782	birth of Nicolo Paganini, famous violinist and composer
1783	Great Britain recognizes United States' independence
1787	U.S. Constitution drawn up
1789	French Revolution begins
1791	Bill of Rights (first 10 amendments of U.S. Constitution) ratified
1793	French King Louis XVI and Queen Marie Antoinette beheaded

For Further Reading

Books for Young Adults

Geras, Adele. *The Random House Book of Opera Stories*. New York: Random House, 1998.

Malem, John. *Wolfgang Amadeus Mozart*. Minneapolis: Carolhoda Books, 1998.

Thompson, Wendy. *Composer's World: Wolfgang Amadeus Mozart*. New York: Viking, 1990.

Ventura, Piero. *Great Composers*. New York: G.P. Putnam's Sons, 1988.

Works Consulted

Anderson, Emily, ed., *Letters of Mozart and His Family*. New York: W.W. Norton, 1986.

Blom, Eric. *Mozart*. Lanham, MD: Littfield, 1978.

Deutsch, Otto Erich. *Mozart: A Documentary Biography*. Stanford, CA: Stanford University Press, 1966.

Einstein, Alfred. *Mozart: His Character, His Work*. New York: Oxford University Press, 1965.

Feldman, David Henry. "Child Prodigies: A Distinctive Form of Giftedness." *Gifted Child Quarterly*, Fall 1993.

Gay, Peter. *Mozart*. New York: Penguin Putnam, Inc., 1999.

Gutman, Robert W. *Mozart: A Cultural Biography*. New York: Harcourt Brace and Co., 1999.

Kolb, Annette. *Mozart*. London: Prion Books Limited, 1937.

Landon, Howard C. Robbins. *Mozart and the Masons*. London: Thames and Hudson, 1991.

Landon, Howard C. Robbins. *Mozart and Vienna*. New York: Schurmer Books, 1991.

Murray, Patrick R., Ken S. Rosenthal, George Kobayashi, et. al. *Medical Microbiology*. St. Louis: Mosby, 1998.

Nardo, Don. *Mysterious Deaths: Mozart*. San Diego: Lucent Books, 1997.

Parouty, Michel. *Mozart: From Child Prodigy to Tragic Hero*. New York: Harry N. Abrams, Inc. 1993.

Sadie, Stanley. *The New Grove Mozart*. New York: W.W. Norton, 1985.

On the Internet

Classical Music Pages: Mozart
    http://w3.rz-berlin.mpg.de/cmp/mozart.html
Lonely Planet: Vienna
    http://www.lonelyplanet.com/destinations/europe/vienna/history.htm
Mozart Biography
    http://www.composers.net/database/m/MozartWA.html
The Mozart Project
    http://www.mozartproject.org
Phoenixmasonry
    http://www.phoenixmasonry.org

Note to Researchers

We know about Mozart's life from the fascinating family letters he left behind, portraits sketched by his contemporaries, and accounts that were written by his relatives, friends, and music critics. These accounts, along with his music, survive today. As with many stories that pass down through time, the mixture of fact and fiction becomes a problem as the years go by. We have tried to consult as many original sources and critical testimony about such sources as possible so as to depict a story about Mozart that is considered accurate by today's standards.

Glossary

archbishop - The highest ranking bishop

aria (ah-REE-ah) - solo song, usually part of an opera

child prodigy (prod-i-GEE) - child who posses a specific talent or skill which is very advanced for his or her age

composer - someone who creates a musical work

concerto (con-CHAIR-toe) - an orchestral piece featuring an instrumental solo

counterpoint - blending of two or more melodies

epidemic (ep-i-DEM-ic) - the rapid spread of a disease

opera (OHP-er-a) - a dramatic work where the actors sing the lines rather than speaking them

patron (PAY-tron) - someone who supports an artist or the arts, usually financially; also called a "sponsor"

Index